How God Prepared And Inspired Me To Be A Writer And Author

Goal: To educate and inspire teenagers (Ages 13-18) to be more spiritual and implement His ways in daily life using a Scripture-based foundation.

Objective: Trace God's creation on how he created me to be a teacher, educator, scientist, and a writer—going back to high-school.

Outcome: The teenagers will learn the importance of:

> *Prayers*
> * *Faith*
> * *Hope*
> * *Patience*
> * *Listening to God's Hidden Messages*
> * *Results of Obeying the Scriptures*

Herbert K. Naito

508 West 26th Street KEARNEY, NE 68848
402-819-3224
info@medialiteraryexcellence.com

Table of Contents

ACKNOWLEDGEMENTS

I want to graciously thank Father Philip Rogers, Pastor of the St. Charles Borromeo Parish, Father Ryan Furlong, Associate Pastor of the St. Charles Borromeo Parish, Deacon Michael Kocjancic of the St. Charles Borromeo Parish, and Deacon Paul Lisko of the St. Charles Borromeo Parish for their diligent and scrutinizing review of this book. Also, thank you for kindness for Blessing this book.

This book was supported by a generous grant from the Dr. and Mrs. Herbert K. Naito Charitable Foundation grant.

CHAPTER 1

INTRODUCTION

When I was developing in the womb of my mother, God already had His own plans as to who and what I was going to be.

> *"Before I formed you in the womb I knew you, and before you were born, I dedicated you, I appointed you a prophet to the nations."*
> *Jeremiah 1:5*

The Lord also promised His commitments to me, forever.

> *"The Lord does not delay his promise, as some regard 'delay', but he is patient with you, and not wishing that any should perish, but that all should come to repentance."*
> *2 Peter 3:9*

> *"The Lord of hosts has sworn: 'As I have planned, so shall it be, and I have purposed, so shall it stand."*
> *Isaiah 14:24*

So, here I am in my graduating high-school gown and have no idea who I am, what I am, and what my future will be. Will I be a pilot? Will I be an engineer? Will I be a doctor? Or will I end up as a homeless vagabond?

I do know that Jesus gave us the freedom of choice—free will for our entire life.

> *"The Lord gave the man this order: you are free to eat from any of the trees of the garden except the tree of knowledge of good and evil"*
> *Genesis 2:16-17*

"The human heart plans the way, but the Lord directs the steps."
Proverbs 16:9

"I will walk freely in an open space because I cherish your precepts."
Psalms 119:45

Not knowing what direction to turn after high-school graduation, my friend told me let's be teachers. So, we both went to one of the best teachers' colleges in USA—University of Northern Colorado. I graduated with a BA and MS degrees in education. I am also certified as a secondary school biological sciences teacher in the state of Colorado.

Again, God prepared me for more writing: writing my Master's degree thesis. However, there were lots of trials and tribulations preparing to be a scholar. I got distracted from God and lost my way by not praying to Him for help and support. Because of my sins, I felt ashamed to ask Him for help.

I went on to the Iowa State University and was awarded a PhD in physiology which provided me with a job at The Cleveland Clinic Foundation in Cleveland, Ohio. Again, more writing training by writing my PhD thesis. Again, like my undergraduate degree, I now felt more ashamed to ask God for forgiveness for my multiple sins because I knew better by the Scripters that I now knew. This degree led to the opportunities of writing 150 scientific papers in medicine. It also, allowed me to pursue my developing passion to be an educator and teacher as Clinical Full Professor in the Graduate School of Chemistry and as Clinical Associate Professor at the Ohio State University School of Medicine. This provided me to refine my communication skills and to express my talents as an educator and scholar by writing lesson plans on different lecture topics.

I spent 15 years at the Veterans Administration Medical Center in Cleveland, Ohio developing a point-of-care department and 14 outpatient clinics writing protocols of different bedside testing procedures for the nurses and medical technologists. My interests in God were renewed and I got back into studying the Bible. A good friend of mine, Doss, from the Jehovah Witness studied the Bible weekly during the summer and fall, using different versions of the different Bibles.

After retirement, what does a person do? Born and raised in Hawaii, I couldn't go deep-sea fishing! Neither could I go surfing! I was lost! Out of the clear-blue sky, one of my best friends said to me, "Herb, you were pretty good at racing at our Cleveland Metro Ski Clubs, which included 26 club race teams. Why don't you teach skiing at the three local ski resorts in Ohio?" Really?

After over 20 years of teaching and educating children, adults, and seniors alpine skiing and writing manuals for my lesson plans for handouts for other ski instructors, I began to realize the journey that God had me on. I delved into the work with a deep passion because I wanted to create happy faces on the slopes. I became 'Pineapple Herb' and was unique and creative. I became an entertainer to create all those happy faces on kids and adults. I did magic tricks, I performed as a ventriloquist with hand puppets, and played the Kazoo on the ride up the chairlift. I even wore a red/green hair wig and other outfits. This effort created a lot of private-lesson requests. I was awarded the *Ski Instructor of the year Award* and the *Franz Bindreiter Award for Dedication to Customer Service*. After serving as director of the Kids Academy for so many years at the three ski schools, now owned by Vail Ski Resorts, one of the two major conglomerates in the ski industry. I decided to retire.

This is a good time to take a break from all these honors and accolades. I was always under the false assumption that through hard work and due diligence, I would achieve these awards. As I studied the Scriptures, I found out that I was WRONG. I was totally wrong! I often time wondered why my Christian friends told me, "Herb, it wasn't you who made all those achievements, it was God!" I now understand the *Truth* and I humbly asked God for forgiveness realizing God gave me those talents and putting them to use for others. Perhaps, this was God's gifts to me through his grace in accordance with his will. Amen.

"For my thoughts are not your thoughts, nor are your ways my ways--oracle of the Lord."

Isaiah 55:8

What should I do when I retired from coaching skiing? Then the pandemic hit. That prompted me to play it safe and start writing because I didn't want to take all the valuable knowledge on skiing to my grave. It is totally selfish! I didn't want to go that route. During my studies, I learned about the importance of sharing and caring while studying the Bible.

"The second is this: you shall love your neighbor as yourself."

Mark 12:31

"For people will be self-centered and lovers of money, proud, haughty, abusive, disobedient to their parents, ungrateful, irreligious, callous, implacable, slanderous, licentious, brutal, hating what is good."

2 Timothy 3:2-4

Do you think that this journey happened haphazardly? Or do you think that it was serendipitous?

There are different pathways that God created:

- To be a writer
- To be an author—to write this book

What do I know about writing books and self-publishing? I have no Idea! But, I said, "With God's help, I'll give it my best effort."

"I will instruct you and show you in the way you should walk, give you counsel with my eye upon you"

Psalm 32:8

The COVID-19 pandemic convinced me to be safe and keep social distance in mind to protect others and keep me safe. I don't have a man cave with soothing background music to accelerate my thought process. What I do have is a large Gazebo outside, surrounded by bright ever- flowing tropical plants (hibiscus, plumeria, roses) and beautiful-smelling shrubs (Gardenia, lavender, lilac) that promote rejuvenation of the mind. It is my sanctuary where I pray and meditate. To be truthful, this is where most of my creative thoughts and ideas about the book come— all from God! Just as Jesus prayed in Garden of Gethsemane, He created my garden (Sanctuary) for beauty and peace; He also provided a space where I can pray and communicate with Him.

I have written 7 other books. Those are:

1. *"A Comprehensive Guide for Coaching Children How to Ski"*

2. *"How To Prepare for Your Child's First Ski Lesson"*

3. *"The Funky Donkey Tells His Story about His First Ski Lesson"*

4. *"Coaching Wacky Raccoon, Children, and Adults the Fundamentals of Good Sportsmanship"*

5. *"The Hidden Secrets of Having Fun At and Around the Ski Resorts"*

6. *"How to Create Fun for Children with Disabilities on the Ski Slopes"*

7. *"How to Create a Successful Ski Lesson for Senior Citizens"*

CHAPTER 2

GOD'S PLANS FOR ME

How was I inspired by God to create ideas and thoughts about writing this book? Well, my thinking was done in the outdoor gazebo, which was my sanctuary. All went well as God gave me thoughts on what to write as I fluently added them to print. But God had other plans in mind. He made it a total struggle to finish the book. I am not the brightest turnip on the wagon when it comes to computer malfunctions! What would you do if you lost a week's worth, a month's worth materials that disappeared into cyberspace?

Many normal individuals would end up angry, depressed, disobedient to God, and saying things that are inappropriate. What it did teach me is I need to have more *perseverance* and *trust* in God.

> *"Consider it all joy, my brothers, when you encounter various trials, for you know that the testing of your faith produces perseverance. And let perseverance have full effect, that you may be perfect and complete, lacking nothing."*
>
> *James 1:2-4*

> *"Trust in the Lord with all your heart, on your own intelligence do not rely; In all your ways be mindful of him, and he will make straight your paths. Do not be wise in your own eyes, fear the Lord and turn away from evil."*
>
> *Proverbs 3:5-7*

In addition, because it went into cyberspace, I determined that God was not pleased with my writing. Sure enough, without complaining when I rewrote the lost files, it ALWAYS came out better! So, there is always a reason for such mishaps. God has His own plans.

What else have I learned from my roller-coaster ride with publishing books with my writings?

One of the most frustrating experience is to forget to *pray* before I start writing. I often underestimate the importance of praying. Praying to God opens our hearts, minds, and souls to Jesus to help grow, change, to love others, and receive His messages. I usually do that every time I visit my sanctuary. Now, it is a ritual.

"Ask and it will be given to you; seek and you will find; knock and it will be opened to you. For everyone who asks receives."
Mathew 7:7-8

Photo 2. A 17-year-old girl praying in church.

Reading the Scripture is filled with prayers to read and learn more about God's ways. This is an area of neglect that we should all re-evaluate our relationship with God. Out of natural survival instinct most of us revert to prayers when we need desperate help. Jesus is seen many times hiding away to pray and even taught His disciples about prayer. He wanted them to learn how to pray the right way. Jesus knew the power and importance of prayer and wanted his disciples to understand this well.

"Therefore, I tell to you, all that you ask for in prayer, believe that you will receive it and shall be yours."

Mark 11:24

Photo 3. A teenager studying the Bible at home.

This brings up the issue of conduct. How are you as a young person to behave? Your center of wisdom and common sense is located in the frontal lobe of the brain. It doesn't fully mature until age 25. That is why so many poor choices are made by teenagers. I highly recommend sticking around people with a good sense of morality and ethical judgement. Going to Christian summer camps, Bible study, and doing missionary work locally and internationally are good ways to enhance your moral compass to always point True North.

"Do not sit with worthless men, nor with hypocrites do I mingle. I hate an evil assembly; with the wicked I do not sit."

Psalm 26:4-5

"Blessed is the man who does not walk in the counsel of the wicked. Nor stand in the way of sinners, nor sit in the company with scoffers. Rather, the law of the Lord is his joy; and on his law he meditates day and night. He is like a tree planted near streams of water, that yields its fruit in season; Its leaves never wither; whatever he does prospers. But not so are the wicked, not so! They are like chaff driven by the wind. Therefore, the wicked will no arise at the judgement, nor will sinners in the assembly of the just. Because the Lord knows the way of the just, but the way of the wicked leads to ruin."

Psalm 1:1-6

"An Eye for an Eye; A tooth for a tooth." Why is there so much hate? Why is there so much wickedness? Why is there so much loath?

Why are there so much *violence* in the streets? Why are teens *harming* each other in the classrooms, schools, malls? Why do they *Bully* each other? Instead, why not pray and let God see the goodness in you and guide you to love, happiness, and kindness? God has unconditional love you and will fulfill your dreams, even in your darkest hour. God's love justifies our lives and fills us with hope for the future. He has great plans for you; so, trust in Him.

"Beloved, let us love one other, because love is of God; everyone who loves is begotten by God and knows God. Whoever is without love does not know God, for God is love."

1 John 4:7-8

"We know that all things together for good for those who love God, who are called according to his purpose."

Romans 8:28

We live in a broken world full of sin and we have free will to make sin-free decisions or they will not be in alignment with God's will. I am certain the causes are multifactorial and there are no simple solutions. However, one major root-reason is the *lack of forgiveness* and *lack of respect for life. Unforgiveness* creates a hardened heart, which feels anger, resentment, bitterness, and hatred toward the offender. Symptoms for unforgiveness:

- You bring anger and bitterness into every relationship and new experience
- You become so wrapped up in the wrong that you can't enjoy the present
- You become depressed and anxious
- You feel that your life lacks meaning or purpose, or that you're at odds with your spiritual beliefs
- You lose the joy of Love for the Lord and for others

There are seven steps to forgiveness:

- Acknowledge the hurt and anger
- Consider how the hurt and pain have affected you
- Accept that you cannot change the past, but you can change the present, and God will change the future
- Acknowledge how your wicked actions has hurt God— your savior
- Release yourself from emotional prison and make a determination to forgive
- Repent
- Continue to pray to receive God's support and grace

There are three types of forgiveness:

1. *Exoneration*: essentially means that the slate is completely wiped cleaned and the relationship is fully restored to its previous sense of innocence. "To forgive and to forget."

2. *Forbearance:* this is a second level forgiveness, which is a partial forgiveness. It is an apology suggesting that the other person is partially to blame for the wrongdoing.

3. *Release:* this is the lowest level of forgiveness, which applies to situations in which the person who hurt you has never acknowledged any wrongdoing. He or she either never apologized or has offered an incomplete or insincere apology. Apology or not, no reparations have been given and the perpetrator has done little or nothing to improve the relationship.

"All bitterness, fury, anger, shouting, and reviling must be removed from you, along with all malice."

Ephesians 4:31-32

"When you stand to pray, forgive anyone against whom you have a grievance, so that your heavenly Father may in turn forgive your transgressions.

Mark 11:25

"Then Peter came to Jesus and asked, 'Lord, how many times shall I forgive my brother or sister who sins against me? Up to seven times?" 'I tell you, not seven times, but seventy-seven times.'

Mathew 18:21-22

Why 77 times? Because He meant to *forgive* with no limits. That is why I always look for the opportunity to ask for God's *forgiveness*. To combat all this strife and anger, we should all work *together*, including teens, and *pray* and *love* our Lord alone. We should all love the Lord our God with all our *heart,* with all our *soul*, with all our *mind,* and with all our *strength*. In addition, we should love our *neighbors* as ourself. There is no other commandment greater than these. *We should ALL LOVE, not hate and harbor anger.*

"You shall love the Lord your God with all your heart, with all your soul, with all your mind, and with all your strength. The second is this: You shall love your neighbor as yourself."

Mark 12:30-31

Photo 4. Teen praying to Jesus Christ

12

Photo 5. Jesus Christ, who we should ALL love with all our heart, with all our soul, with all our mind, and with all our strength

I personally, also follow the motto: What Would Jesus Do (WWJD)? I live my life daily to demonstrate my leadership in the community as a follower of God's Commandments. It is presumptuous to assume what Jesus Christ would do, but I do want to follow His teachings of *Love* and *Mercy* in the Gospel. I am committed to this mode of behavioral conduct by wearing a bracelet to remind me each day how I will execute my thoughts and actions according to my learning of the Gospel. According to God, we need to carry our own cross daily. Jesus looks at his disciples and tell them "Whoever want to be my disciple must deny themselves and take up their cross and follow me."

"Then he said to all, "If anyone wishes to come after me, he must deny himself and take up his cross daily and follow me."
Luke 9:23

13

But, what about the future? How do I face the uncertain future, which may be froth with danger, diseases, chronic pain, death? God has plans for everyone—for welfare and not for evil.

"For I know well the plans I have in mind for you—oracle of the Lord—plans for your welfare and not for woe, so as to give you a future of hope. When you call me, and come and pray to me, I will listen to you. When you look for me, you will find me. Yes, when you seek me with all your heart, I will let you find me—oracle of the Lord—and I will change your lot; I will gather you together from all the nations and all the places to which I have banished you—oracle of the Lord—and bring you back to the place which I have exiled you."
Jeremiah 29:11-14

So, praying to Jesus with all my heart will bring me hope for the future. I must continue to pray daily and have faith in Christ. But what happens if my cross is too heavy to carry? According to the Scriptures, that will never happen.

"No trial has come to you but what is human. God is faithful and will not let you be tried beyond your strength; but with the trial he will also provide a way out, so that you may be able to bear it."
1 Corinthians 10:13

We must all remember that we are all sinners. That is why God sacrificed His one and only begotten Son on the cross for us sinners. We should all be grateful for this sacrifice and respect his genuine love for us.

"For God so loved the world, that He gave His only Son, so that everyone who believes in Him will not perish, but have eternal life. For God did not send the Son into the world to judge the world, but so that the world might be saved through Him."
John 3:16-17

CHAPTER 3
WHAT GOD IS TRYING TO TEACH ME

In addition to what I mentioned in the previous chapters, I think that God is trying to teach me the importance of the following:

- The importance of daily Bible
- study The importance of daily
- praying The importance of
- believing in God The importance of Trusting in God
- The importance of having Faith in God
- The importance of being humble and respecting God as the all-powerful being
- God created everything for you
- Evangelize the Gospel
- The importance of following the 10 Commandments
- The importance of forgiving
- The importance of demonstrating Christian behavior

Photo 6. The New American Bible.[a]

_____

[a] *All-Biblical quotes were taken from this Bible.*

CHAPTER 4

SUMMARY

This has been a long journey writing this book for me. God has taught me so much about my deficiencies while going through the trials and tribulations of this manuscript. Carrying the Cross is not easy and will not be easy in the future. Christ, I think, has narrowed my path and has made it is much straighter to reach paradise. The impact of this authorship journey opened new doors for me. It gave me the knowledge to be humble enough to make the necessary changes to be what God expects. My new goal is to share my new inspirations about having a *closer* relationship with Jesus by reading and mediating the Scriptures and applying it to everyday life. I will preach the Gospel and every once- in-awhile, I will vocalize my thoughts to others. I am hopeful that this book will help inspire others to be a better Christian. May your life be Blessed with God's Blessings.

Photo 7. Picture of St. Charles Borromeo Parish

REFERENCE

1. The New American Bible, revised edition; Confraternity of Christian Doctrine, Inc; Washington, DC; 2010, 1430 pages.

ABOUT THE AUTHOR

He spent 40 years in the medical profession. For fun, he coached skiing for over 20 years. He is a member of the Professional Ski Instructors of America, and is certified in Alpine Skiing, Level 2; Adaptive Specialist, Level 1; Children's Specialist, Level 2; Children's Trainer; and Senior Specialist, Level 2. Currently, he is employed by Vail Resorts and is presently on the Vail Educational Staff. He was the former Director of the Children's Advanced Training Specialist and the Express Pre-School School Ski Programs.

www.ingramcontent.com/pod-product-compliance
Lightning Source LLC
Chambersburg PA
CBHW081543120626
46550CB00009B/2843